POEMS
&
PROSE
OF ATONEMENT

BART KEEGAN

Poems & Prose of Atonement
© 2018 Bart Keegan

trabkeegan@talktalk.net
biomediaworx.com/bartkeegan

ISBN (hardcover): 978-1-7364497-5-2
ISBN (paperback): 978-1-7364497-6-9
ISBN (Amazon paperback): 979-8-2649912-0-2
ISBN (ebook, all formats): 978-1-7364497-7-6

Published by
Bio Mediaworx
P.O. Box 1233
Liberty, MO 64069
U.S.A.

WORKS

Diary of Atonement: The case for good and evil

Poems & Prose of Atonement

Wittgenstein's Philosophical Investigations:
Identity as Paradox

CONTENTS

THE SIGH

Or did I sigh
Just now?
When I awakened from
My sleep
Of death
Into the channel of
The nightened day
In fright?
As when I saw you
Passing by
Just now
Beneath my feet
And underneath my head
Of clay

So stay!

O golden clamour of the day
That rattles, stirs, begets the way
Of loving life, yet lived
Astride your mighty sway!

GRAND DAMES EXIST

Grand Dames exist
To stir the cauldron of my soul
To crow in coarseness
Curses to bestow
And with their blackened robes and
Skinny hands,
Repulsive faces
Wicked yellow'd teeth
And cackled laughs,
Grand Dames exist
To guide us into
Hell

Or should I tell?
Of new beginnings from this final hour
Their bower
Encapsulating me
That I might suffocate in agony
To death
To be delivered from and by
The hands of these Grand Dames
Of Old
A next new seed to be?

GEORGE BEST IS DEAD

He died at last
They mourn him now
He's in a box and
On TV
The only one that's there
That cannot hear

George Best

PLAY THE DAY AWAY

All things considered —
The world turns on its axis
And flies live only the length
Of a summer

And Gods rise out of the

So let the woman be
And see her child appear
Born new

For Gods rise out of the

So play
The day
Away

4

ON A HILLTOP DAY

For all I see
The roses seem to bloom
For all I know
The life is doom and gloom
For all I want
Is Time to end
And this to never be
For all I care
The fox runs sly
And wily to its lair
Up in the skies
The mounting clouds ahigh
With lifting rapture
Of my heart as sure
I feel
The nearness of
You die
Within me
To be ever born anew

For all I love
It never is enough
For all I ache
To see you in the
Buff

I live and long and thrill
To be
With you. Again.
For all I see to be

ANGELS NEVER DANCE

Angels never dance with me
You know
Their wings when even folded
Get in the way
Of my crushing hot embrace
As I attempt
To glide them 'cross the ballroom
In my sway

They hover
Never touch their feet
On to this clay
Of mine

But I will be
Their death
You wait and see
For in atoning for my sins
Of scarlet
Splattered on the snow
I'll bury God and then at last be free
So angels then all gone can never dance with me

THE NEARLY MAN

Today I saw the Nearly Man
Nearly for an hour
He ski'd his way into my
Life
Singing songs of Rome
And warm'd with wine
From wineskins

Oh Nearly Man
Resurrect my life
As you know how
Tingle me with gladness
Of your smile
So nearly, now

I fell in love
It seems
I cried with shouts of joy
And exultation
Carol was my song
Of day

Oh Nearly Man!
Oh, Nearly, Nearly, King of kings, Divine!

8

I SHADOW IN YOUR NAME

How high do sound the
Sounds of heaven
In my heart
How thunderous the
Roar of thunder
In my veins
How wild the winds of
March do blow across
My vision
How dance the dancing
Flames of love
Within my breast

And did you come to me
In dreams last night?
And did you run to me
With open arms?
And did your eyes ope wide
With lights of love?
And did you speak my name
In whispered joy?

Oh how the sounds of heaven
Fill my heart!
Oh how the thunder of your sweetness
Sounds through my veins!
Oh how the March winds bluster at
My eyes of tear-filled joy!
Oh how the dancing flames of life
Rage lovely in my breast!

Ah love divine — I shadow

In your name

ANY ROAD

Down our road
Death's died
It happened one o'clock
Last Monday morning

And all the lights
Came on
Doors opened
Out stepped feet
Bodies swayed with
Joy
Dancing, we surveyed
The stars
The silver of the moon
And context dark
Of heavens

Down our road
Death's died

So now we're shining —
Lighting up the stars
And silvering the moon —
A thing we always did
And never knew

NOTES OF A MADLY LOVING PERSON

The logic's gone
The mind is spent
All reason's lost
The rationale just went
Its way

Today
The curtains have divided
And into view another
Logic heaves
And breathes
Another life to me
Another me

A madly loving person's
Come to stay
Has carried me away
Into cradle's gold
Of old
It knew me and
I never guessed

Sit palpitating fast
My heart
Stand stiff the hairs
At back of neck

Death's here
At last
A madly, madly, madly, loving person

IN FIELDS OF GOLD

In fields of gold
Where lie the lilies low
And stand the sunflowers
Tall
I spent my summer's days
In murmur of a land
I used to know
A land beyond recall

There in that land
Amidst its pastured hills
And valley floors
I ran
As boyhoods do on boyhood days
Drinking from the babble of
Its brooks
Its crystal waters clear
And seeing with the eye
What eyes of loveliness alone
Do see

Your face

And in the wind that called
To me
Wresting movements from my tresses
Filling me with grace
I lay at last beneath a knotted oak
Warm and succoured sweet
In your embrace

(repeat first verse)

MY BERNADETTE MARY

In the cooling beauty of the night
I see your face
In the warming sunlit day
I feel your close embrace
In the waters of the streams
I see your dancing eyes
As in the landscape of my dreams
Your memory never dies

THE KISS

Turning now to thoughts of love
I bring to mind your smile
Your lovely voice and soft brown eyes
That make my life worthwhile
The magic of your hand in mine
My lips on yours divine
To change our friendship into love
Like water into wine

GOLD OF SHE

Bright gold is the colour of my life
When I hold you in embrace
Gold is the colour of my day
Whene'er I see your face
And when you smile the smile of love
At me
My heart adores its
Magicality
Leaving me enwrapped
In mystery
Of why it's my life that you choose
Enfolding it in gold

THE FACE

I know a lady
Five foot one
She gives me love amazing
And at her lovely
Photo face
I'm secretively gazing

THE MEN WHO INHABIT CAFES

The men who inhabit cafes
In rumpled macs and
Shoes worn thin
Of leather
Cragged faces
Shagged out faces
But busy with their food
Ravenously chewing
Gorging full on chips and
Peas
And parts of cooked dead
Animals
Their kin
And lounging fatly on his
Thank-you-for-your-custom
Counter
Our friend ubiquitous chef
Surveying men who eat his
Food
Noting grubby marks of grubby hands
Imprinted in the grease- veneer

Of table-cloths
Check-red
And somewhere in the haze of
Fatty acid air
The dead
Quite dead
Needing only to do the deed
Of dying

These men who inhabit cafes

At the dawning of each day
I try my hardest not to pray
Why should God get all the praise
What about me —
When I can't find a word
To rhyme with praise?

THE UNRESOLVED

Dark tragedy Thou
Whene'er did I see you
Whene'er did I not?

Thou, my diadem, my crowning thorn
Toss'd upon this sea I am
And Thou?

Begone!

Thou art my bitter cup, my blood
And in this agony
Forever I must as must go on
In Death

O Thou!

Whens't dids't Thou spy me —
As a babe?
Thought Thou I'll take him
Make him
For my own!

O damn'est curse!
Dark tragedy
Thou

THE KISS ON THE ASS

Ride me
Prisoners of the dawn
And I will carry you
As seated on your ass
My ass
Will travel forth
To take you to your
Third hour afternoon
Communion
Face to face
And ass to ass
Your night with day
Will there abide
In grace

NEW BEGINNINGS

The leaf unfurls
So slow at first it hardly moves
At all
Into the light of life

Petals, they unfold, unfurl
To find the Muse beholding them
And making them
Her own

I curse
The curse is but a seed
Once sown
Yields life
Unto its own

O how I cry
To Thee
Grand Mother, Muse of all creation
To take me
Make me
Nothing
Life full-blown

I hardly move, I wait
My new beginnings in the life of old

OH FOLLY

Folly be mine!
And take me
For thine own!
Full wed are we
As on our steed of life
We charge beneath the moon
Into the gold of day
And out across the plains
Ride free!

And me?

I watch

The third one
Of the three

CONSTRAINTS UPON MY SOUL

Constraints upon my soul are few
And yet so many
Imprisoned as I am
In cast of clay
Am I to say
What is, or was, or is to be?
Or am I cast a role
To mute with worry stay?
Constraints
They fetter me
My sister soul, she lies in dudgeon deep
Whilst I, her brother earth
A brooding, darkest, deepest watch do keep

YOUR FACE IS ALL I SEE

We never knew the games we played
We never knew the score
We danced about the midnight bower
And Wizard held the floor
We never knew the laughter
We never knew the sighs
We used to run and hide away
And Wizard held the skies
Or was it rumoured long ago
And was it told abroad
That dancers, on the midnight hour,
In Wizard are restored
I loved you then
I love you now
I'll love for evermore
I want to tell
Of hearts of gold
I've known
Adored
And lost
To your

Embrace
Your face
Is all I see
Before me now
As slowly I ascend
To face my death, another life
With you to daily spend

TO BARBY

If I had my way
And the starlight were mine
I'd save it to shine from my eyes
With devotion so true
And only for you
Til my heart stops its beating
And dies
Then I'll climb Jacob's ladder
And be that much gladder
If you'll come with me
Up to the skies
And there in the clouds
We'll cast off our shrouds
Of sorrow, of sadness
And sighs

MAGNIFICENT FOREBODINGS

Master
What are you doing there
Beneath my toe?

So slow are you
To catch my fire of night
So slight a frame
You cast
Beneath my bow

O rainbows never last
Yet spring
Eternal into sight
That only you
Behold

Magnificent forebodings
Thou hast me by
The throat
And with same knife
Cut then thou my gizzard
Slit it, slow
For quickened life like blood
From me to flow

GENTLENESS

On still, warm, days
Days drenched with perfume of the honeysuckle
My tender skin as soft as petal of
The rose
I think of you
See you soft recumbent
Languorously
And shout with pinnacle of joy
With zenith cry of gladness
Rushing headlong as a child
Falling to my knees to greet you
Raised on yours
And there we stun in rapturous embrace
Deep kissings
Hearts on fire with love
Honey-clothed in gentleness

All this .....
And more .....
My Darling love

On still, warm, days

EVER ANGEL EYES

Ever angel eyes which
Change for me though
You be on the page as
Literature
And I be in the chair
Behind the pen

Oh ever angel eyes I
Come to you
Astride a snail
No ordinary snail —
A racing snail
Now with you in a trice yet
Ever racing to you
Ever Ever
Ever angel eyes

OH, LITTLE STAR

Tarry little star of love
Oh, tarry now
Begin descent from velvet black of night
Earthward travel
Hover over me
And light upon my brow

Ah Prince of light
Oh lovely little star
My shining hope
Thou light on me
Yea settle on my brow
And when the life eternal comes my way
Be thou my diadem
My princely crown

For ever have I loved and searched for thee
In all the days I've counted on this earth
And ever hast thou been a friend to me
Beginning from the moment of my birth

Ah, little star of hope
Oh light of love
Tarry in the heavens
Wait for me
If thou descendest not, I will arise to thee
And we shall kiss in brightest light
Our final kiss of ecstasy

YOUR MAN

In the winter's night of long ago
When babies slept and mothers at the hearth-side sewed
When men betook to drinking and alehouse liquor flowed

And dogs howled
In the night

I came to you
And you said Yes
And there we passed each night away
In sinful state
Until the early cockerel crowed

Then,
Spent of love
I over fields and fences went
Towards my home
Arriving as the breakfast-meal
Was being laid
And never did my mother question why
Or where I'd gone
But looked, instead

Into my eyes and with her love
Forgave

Oh winter's summer days
When I gave up my being just her child
And took to learning how to be
Your man

JANET

I know a lady, nicely small
A mine of information
She gives me facts and that's not all
Then sees me to the station

We walk the dog
And talk a lot
And nothing seems to matter
As God stops work –
An ear for love –
To listen to our chatter

Shining heart
With passion in its pay
I give to you
Like apple on a tray

God made the world
And named the flowers
But Bart forgot the names
So Janet censured — just a bit -
But still gave Bart his games

What do you come here for?
(Janet made him tell)
And do you like it lots of times?
(He'd answered rather well)

Feel no more the heat of the sun
Its warming days are over
Just bed with me and have some fun
Let heartshine be the clover
Can I do you now Miss?
Though day has just begun
I have to quench a fire you see
That's hotter than the sun

There's Celtic Welsh, a Davies girl
A sex-appealing wench
And Irish Celt, a Keegan man
Who kisses her in french

Hey Ho! The livelong day!
It's naughty time again
Show me something I can have
And I'll soon put down this pen!

Kisses here, kisses there
Kisses on my letter
But kisses tucked up warm in bed
Are perfect, if not better!

This telephone number of mine
Is waiting for calls on the line
From my number one choice
Yes, a Janet whose voice
I can listen to time upon time

I like to visit Milton Keynes
I come back feeling grateful
Aquarian romance I do find
— Its spell on me is fateful

I like to be a good boy
A good boy
A good boy
I like to be a good boy
If I can
But when I am a naughty boy
A naughty boy
A naughty boy
I'm spanked and kissed
And loved to death
And helped to be a man

There's two mice in the cupboard
Miss Janet, Miss Janet
There's two mice in the cupboard
Oh dear

They're having a poke
And it's far from a joke
For Pied Pipers these days
Cost so dear

I'm a complicated gentleman
Ambivalent and fickle
But Irish Catholic t'be sure
So I like my slap and tickle

I'll come to see your new settee
And watch a bit of tele
Then off to bed
To rest my head
Upon your saucy belly

MY FATHER

Can I forget that once we walked together
Your face is here within a heart of tears
Fond mem'ry holds the door for you companion
To render Time unconscious of the years

Now I can bring to mind your talk and laughter
The antics of a man beyond his prime
And now the trace of peace about your features
Your handshake of farewell to earthly time

We all are what we are because of others
And I remain forever in your debt
So fare thee well for still I have the mem'ry
Of how that once upon a time we met

MR MERRYWEATHER

Mr Merryweather
In the morning of his life
Stepped out of his suburban door and —
With bowler carefully set
Upon his head —
Strolled forth
Along suburban pavements
Which he measured walked
To catch the 8.15
Suburban local train
Into the city
Quite unmindful
On the way
Of gaping crevice opened up
Behind his leisured measured gait
Said later to have been
A chasm due to subsidence
Yet tho' it yawned
Into a depth quite bottomless
Our Mr Merryweather
Noting carefully the joy of life
And song of love

44

For all things of that bright and sunny
Newest day
Had no such ken of
Things behind
Much less of their calamitous
Significance
But — more akin to Lot
Than Mrs Lot —
Our hero never looked
To other than his front
And so continued on his
Morning routine walk to
Board the train
For London

Yet scarce had Mr Merryweather
Taken twice a score
Of further paces forward than
Directly at his back —
As he had conscientious halfway crossed
A road held clear for him by
Lights at red —
A double decker local bus
Glided dangerously past
Having totally ignored the red
Stop sign
Its driver dead behind the

Wheel

In sudden silent fatal heart attack

But all our praises let us sing to

Mr Merryweather

For his love of life

Such that he could be so forward looking and

In blissful total unawaredness of things behind his

Back

And more — as if this had not been

Enough —

When approximately

Never further than a throw of stone away

From station entrance

Mr Merryweather

Goodness me

Passed across a spot upon the pavement's flagstone

Aimed for by a lady who

At that very point in time

Was falling to her

Death

From out an upper storey window

Of a high rise building where

She worked as cleaner — supposed

That day to be engaged in

Polishing the windows but

Fell out

By mishap so it seems as
Was reported in the later "Evening News"
All credit to our Mr Merryweather
Who — though she fell in huddled
Thump
Behind his back ...
Proceeded onward
Eyes to front
The soul of bright rejoicings
At the day that lay ahead

How wonderful
A thing
Suburban life
Uneventful for the
Mr Merryweathers
Of our world who
Living there
Can feel the blessedness
Of all things bright and beautiful
Simply on account
Of forward-facing inclinations
Never blighted
By things past

Their hymn to life

THE CHILD

I was thinking of my mum, the other day. I was remembering how devoted a Catholic she was and how devout a child I was. I was so holy that three times a day God used to pray to *me*. Anyway, I used to love those early mornings of my mother waking me at six and we setting out for the Mass & Holy Communion, every day. I loved it. I used to love the early hour and the world so still and so incredibly beautiful and my having my adored mother all to myself. I think I've told you before but I so truly adored my mum that, compared to me, Oedipus was a misogynist.

I used to bob along beside her, holding her hand, just a little boy of seven or so, and I used to drink in everything she told me about when she was a little girl. I used to ferment with endless questions and whenever I'd ask something like, "And do you miss Grandma now she's gone to heaven, mummy?" she'd use her old-Irish-wise-way-of-murmuring to me, "I do child, I do."

My heart used to sing of beauty as I looked up into her face and my eyes always saw the most beautiful mother in the world. She was my first and greatest love and that remained the case until my love of loves came into my life. Yet even today and though she now has left this world I adore my mother.

Those were days of hope. The German war had just ended. Everywhere along the route to our local district church of the Sacred Heart there was evidence of the German blitz on Coventry which, like the London docklands of the east end, was one of Hitler's prime targets. Night after night the waves of bombers came. I remember all too well the sound of the heavy, steady, and relentless drone of the night-time bombers as we waited below, a family of love-twinned-with-terror, to see where the horrendous bomb-blast would occur. But those earlier memories were softened in the aftermath of the war as I sped along with my mum to the church of the Sacred Heart. Complete houses were missing. Debris lay in vast piles. Single end-walls of houses stood solitary to the open sky and remnants of upstairs bedroom-wallpaper covered such solitary walls while set up absurdly high in the wall was the small, iron, bedroom fireplace grate.

A cat would be seen, picking its way over the rubble, testing out each loose brick fragment with a soft cat-paw before giving its weight to the debris. Folk passed each other in the street & looked fleetingly at one another from bright eyes of hope set in white faces of strain and the eyes asked one another the same question: "Can it be over? Can it be over? Can it be over?"

In the aftermath of war I wore grey, as did all of the children. True, on Sundays I had my Sunday suit of blue with jacket and short trousers and blue-grey socks and black shoes. I was a very pretty boy especially in my Sunday suit with white shirt and little red tie. But in the week we were grey. And unpretty.

Yes, they were days of hope. And days of happiness. And as I journeyed back & forth, back & forth, to the early morning masses at the little church I grew in wisdom of the ways of men and how deeply little boys can love. I forgot for a while, when I became a dad. But its etched again now on my heart.

Well, the summer passed. There was a big street party to celebrate the end of the war. The schools re-opened and we returned to tend our lessons, learn how to do real joined-up writing, play conkers in the autumn play-ground, pray at night for the souls of the dead, & squabble over the breakfast table for the last piece of fried-bread. And winter came. I recall feeling devastated when my big sister forgot and left her pet water-beetle out in the garden overnight & there it was frozen solid in ice next day. We used to blow on our hands with the cold and think it fun to get our little bottles of frozen school milk to drink on the school verandah with our bit of lunch. I saw God in everything and wanted to be a priest so I could get picked by God to be a saint. It was a child's world. The war was over. And everything seemed possible.

OF SOME

Of some there are
In wakened dreams
Epic stories of grand strength
Of fortitude
And courage spent
Of gold that glisters
Hair unkempt

The children never question
The children never shout
The children drink the man of truth
And grow to live without

But of some
The histories expand and swell
With pride
With unquestioning belief
And loyalties as fierce as any dog
Of Sykes

The children never question
And grow to live without

SUSAN

In the mirrors of the night
Down the hallways draped in time
Ever new in crystal sadness
Thirsts the warrior in the child

Never fleeting was her moment
Never lost her footing sure
Ever in a crowd of angels
Sang she of her widow's curse

Came the moment, came the crisis
Shrunken old her nightless soul
Bold her brazened limbs of honey
Bright the chuckles of her glee

Forward into life becoming
Never seen before nor known
Stepped she as a new creation
And all journeys met
Foretold

SACKCLOTH JOHN

Sackcloth John, a man I used to know
Wore his ashes on his head
Iron-grey
That'll be the day, I told myself
That I should be like him

And the seasons changed
The violet years rolled by
And not content with waiting
Fell to wondering why
Was it all a waste?
Where were we bent, by God?

Years later
I saw John again
Shuffling broken-backed along the street
I fell upon my knees, cried 'Lord!'
Just as John turned
My life away from his
With sparkling ease

BRIGHT DAY

Bright day
I've loved you since
The end of time
You know

You know

That honour'd bible knowledge
Once again

To love
To intercourse
Have dealings of a
Non-specific kind
As does the blackning dark of night
With mistress golden day

Bright day
I thank you for your chat
And though full groped yet
Hungering still for more
I'll be content
And leave it now, at that

COVENANT

Of worries wearing
Thin the page
I stand
Full blast
In covenant with death

O yes
In covenant with death
I stand

At last

In covenant with death I stand
To hand
The resurrection
And something in between I s'pose
For my repose
Dark soul of night

In covenant with death I stand
At brink of milky dew of dawn
A harvest of the past
At last
Now done with writing out
Vast literature

NOTES UPON A SUMMER'S DAY

And on a summer's day
Are these
Notes upon
And a
And summer's
And day
That's all I hear
Of these
The tunes of loveliness
These notes of thine my
Notes
Upon a summer's day
And on a summer's day

MY MOTHER

When evening shadows lengthen
And quiet grows the day
I think of you and send you love
With words that ever say
God keep you safe and bless you
And fill your heart with joys
The way you filled your married life
With endless girls and boys

TIME

Time awakes the workers
Wrenching them from sleep
And pours them onto pavements
Garbed in grey
To throng in crowds
And mute with worry weep
At passing time that wastes the day away

But stop and think
For Time is not the foe
Nor is there need to feel by it oppress'd

For Time is born of woman
And beats within the breast
It cloaks itself in human form
And lays itself to rest

ABOUT THE AUTHOR

Bart Anthony Keegan, Ph.D., lives quietly in London pursuing his foremost interest: the philosophy of suffering. During his sojourns in England and Australia, he studied divinity and philosophy and began to question the meaning of life, the sense that theologians and philo-sophers made of it. This interest gradually focused on how to think about anything at all and the logic that is used as the tool of thinking. Bart met up with Anselm's proof for the existence of God and this changed entirely the direction of his interest. In that moment, he began to question if the way we think is in need of radical change from the root: the axioms of thought themselves.

The Diary of Atonement, *Poems & Prose of Atonement*, and *Identity as Paradox* are the fruit of Bart's questioning: They offer up as their thesis that each identity–person or thing–in the story of the world is an atonement of opposites: a paradox, from which, Bart came to understand that suffering, as sorrow, together with its opposite such as glory qua that which is glorious are cases as paradoxically one another, where their paradox case as their common identity case is neither one of them but both of them at once, and this (borrowing from Anselm) as that than which nothing greater can be conceived–identity-as-paradox as, so to call it, creativity as such. Each identity in the story of the world is a creativity, presenting either wholly negatively, wholly positively, or by turns each of these opposites. By which, that which is called the problem of evil–here called the problem of suffering–is accounted for as warranted by the justice of creativity as such, the fruits of which thereby are the cases of good and evil, glory and suffering, rejoicing and sorrow—the head-and-tail faces, so to speak, of the coin of untold measure that is identity as paradox.

Bart invites discussion regarding his work:
trabkeegan@talktalk.net

ABOUT THE DESIGNER

Elizabeth Beeton is a jill of all trades and mistress of none. Her life is mundane, made up of the usual things many humans experience: marriage, kids, ailing parents, aging, failing health, church, in-laws, outlaws, and scrabbling for a living.

She lives in Kansas City, Missouri, USA, writes novels, and is the owner of **B10 Mediaworx**, an author publishing services company. She designs print books, ebooks, and book covers. She publishes her own novels under the B10 Mediaworx imprint, and literature in a niche religious genre under the Peculiar Pages imprint. They don't make any money, but they are works that deserve a place in the Library of Congress. She builds and maintains her own websites.

She has a bachelor's in English, creative writing and journalism, from the University of Missouri at Kansas City.

She also reads, organizes her office endlessly, and tinkers on her computer (sometimes to ill effect). She's a fair-weather

Kansas City Chiefs and Royals fan, half-arsed planner, avid cross stitcher, dilettante crafter, and aspiring odalisque. She regularly thumbs her nose at her to-do list as if it has any authority over her at all. Her life's goal is to finish all the craft projects she has ever begun. *All* of them.

biomediaworx.com